MY FAMILY TREE WORKBOOK
Genealogy for Beginners

Rosemary A. Chorzempa

DOVER PUBLICATIONS, INC., NEW YORK

*To all my ancestors I have come to know, love,
and understand through family history research.*

Copyright © 1982 by Rosemary A. Chorzempa.
All rights reserved under Pan American and International Copyright Conventions.

Published in Canada by General Publishing Company, Ltd.,
30 Lesmill Road, Don Mills, Toronto, Ontario.
Published in the United Kingdom by Constable and Company, Ltd.,
3 The Lanchesters, 162–164 Fulham Palace Road, London W6 9ER.

My Family Tree Workbook: Genealogy for Beginners is a new work,
first published by Dover Publications, Inc., in 1982.

International Standard Book Number: 0-486-24229-3
Library of Congress Catalog Card Number: 81-67628

Manufactured in the United States of America
Dover Publications, Inc.
31 East 2nd Street
Mineola, N.Y. 11501

Preface

A family tree is an illustration that shows how a person is linked by blood or marriage to his or her relatives, whether living or dead. Genealogy is the science of determining who belongs on a particular family tree. Genealogy is interesting in its own right: all of us want to know who our relatives are. It is also important for certain legal matters. For example, genealogy plays an important role in the laws concerning inheritance. Since most property is handed down from one generation to the next, it is necessary to know who is related to whom, and which relationships are the closest. In cases where the line of descent is not clear, a genealogist may be called in to determine who is the closest relative of someone who died and left behind some property. Genealogy is also important in countries such as England where there is a hereditary aristocracy whose members are entitled to special privileges simply by virtue of their birth. Kings, princes, dukes, and barons are all hereditary aristocrats. Sometimes people try to falsify their family connections in order to inherit property they are not entitled to, or because they want the status of being part of a distinguished family. It is the duty of the genealogist to make sure that the family tree is drawn accurately: false or artificial branches are unacceptable.

My Family Tree Workbook is an introductory workbook in genealogical research. It is meant to be a gateway to further study. It is designed especially for young people, but adults with no previous experience in this field may find it useful. Anyone as young as ten years can begin this work and follow up on more detailed aspects of genealogy at the end of the book at a later time. Parents are a valuable source of information for the genealogy student. Family involvement is almost a necessity for this workbook, since genealogy is family history.

After you complete this book you may expand your research into other areas. I have included some suggestions for further research in the sections Where to Get Help, More Things to Do, and Books to Help You.

Although most of the material in this book assumes that all relationships are "full," you may have "half" or "step" relations. If you and your brother have the same mother and father, then your brother is a *full brother*. When one parent in a family dies, or when the parents in a family get divorced, a second family may be started. The children in the second family are the *half brothers* and *half sisters* of the children in the first family—half, not full, because only one parent is shared. If a parent remarries after either a divorce or the death of a spouse, that parent's second spouse becomes the *stepfather* or *stepmother* of the children from what we are calling the first marriage. The stepfather or stepmother may have had children from a previous marriage; these children are *stepbrothers* and *stepsisters* of the children from the first marriage. If you have half or step relations, you may wish to make special entries on the workbook pages to include all of your relatives. You may find this form to be useful:

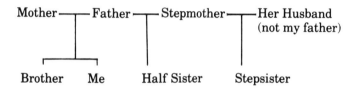

The short horizontal line between a man and a woman indicates a marriage.

A word on abbreviations. Many abbreviations are used in genealogy. Some of the very common ones are listed below. You may wish to use them yourself to save time and space.

b.	= Born
m.	= Married
d.	= Died
bd.	= Buried
bap.	= Baptized
c.	= Circa
NMI	= No middle initial

Circa means "about," as in "c. 1875," which means "about (the year) 1875." *NMI* means "No middle initial." You might see "John NMI Doe" on a document.

You may also wish to invent a few more abbreviations for your own convenience for words that you are using a lot. Keep a list of abbreviations for you to remember and for others who will be reading your work.

When writing dates, never use numbers to abbreviate the months. For example, don't use 2/7/51 for February 7, 1951. It might get confused with 2 July 1951. Instead, use either the standard form (February 7, 1951) or the form preferred by genealogists (7 February 1951) in this order: day/month/year.

Contents

Climbing Your Family Tree

The best way to find out about your family history is to start with yourself. That's why there are so many questions about you in this book. You have to know yourself first, then you can use what you have found out to reach out into other areas.

The next step is to talk to your parents, grandparents, aunts, and uncles. Take notes of the important facts. You might like to use a tape recorder when talking to your relatives—so that nothing is forgotten—but ask their permission first. Always write down who gave you the information and the date. Someone who gives you information is called a *source*. Never rely on anyone's memory for accurate data. Later you can verify the data you have heard by locating the proper records, which your public library can help you find.

Keep a notebook. A loose-leaf binder works best. Have a page for each of your relatives, and include everything you have heard from them or about them, especially vital data such as dates of births, marriages, and deaths and where these events took place. When you obtain a vital record or official document, enter all the information on the proper person's sheet. Note the source, certificate number, county, state or province, and so on. (See the Sample Page of Notebook Filing System that appears later in the book.) Always use a pencil if you are not sure the information you are entering is correct. When you are certain that it is correct, use ink. This practice will keep your papers neat.

Find a box or expandable folder for storing copies of vital records, important papers, and photographs. Use manila folders or large envelopes for the different categories.

Your grandparents or your great-grandparents, if they are living, are probably your best source of family information. They can be especially helpful in the ethnic sections of this book. Remember, they were once young too, and they will enjoy telling stories about their youth to interested young people.

When you visit relatives, ask them to show you their photo albums, scrapbooks, family bibles, baby books, and news clippings. Be sure to bring along your own photo albums to show them. They will then feel more certain that you are willing to exchange information with them, rather than feel that you want to use them only for your own purposes.

You will probably spend much time in your library's local history and genealogy departments. There is much information there that can help you in your search. The holdings in different libraries vary, so check out several libraries in nearby cities. Don't be afraid to ask librarians for help—that's what they are there for—but don't expect them to do all your work for you. Additional places to look for help can be found in the section Where to Get Help.

You can use many of the subjects you learned in school for genealogy. Some of these are geography, United States and world history, local (state or province, county, and city) history, government, and foreign languages. Even knowledge of your family's religion and economics, psychology, and logic is helpful. To succeed in discovering your family tree, you must like detective work, and talking with people, especially older ones. You must be very tactful and courteous.

You may come upon conflicting information from different sources. This conflict could have arisen from different spellings of names, different dates or ages, faulty memories, and similar things. The best thing to do is to write down each variation and who your source was. You may or may not eventually find out which version is correct.

Do not be discouraged if you find that results take a long time or that you seem to be getting nowhere. Put your work away for a while and come back to it later. Time brings out fresh ideas. It may take years to accumulate a sizable amount of information. You will never be completely finished. Your family tree goes back on and on and on.

Me

Photo
here

Name _____

Nickname _____

Address:

   Number and street _____

   City and county _____

   State or province and Zip Code _____

Date family research was started _____

Father's name _____

Mother's name _____

Social Security Number _____

Color of eyes _____ **Color of hair** _____

Hobbies and sports _____

_____

_____

Interesting facts about me _____

_____

_____

_____

_____

_____

_____

_____

My Beginning

Date of birth _____

Time of birth _____

Place of birth:

  Name of hospital _____

  City and county or province _____

  State and Zip Code _____

My doctors _____

_____

Weight at birth _____ Length at birth _____

Whom I was named after _____

Baby photo here

Paste a copy of your birth certificate, your birth announcement card, or a newspaper clipping announcing your birth here.

Places Where I Have Lived

Address of my present home:

Number and street _____

City and county _____

State or province and Zip Code _____

Years lived here _____

Addresses of my previous homes:

Number and street _____

City and county _____

State or province and Zip Code _____

Years lived there _____

Number and street _____

City and county _____

State or province and Zip Code _____

Years lived there _____

Paste in photos of your homes. Then draw a map of your state and show where your present home is located.

My Religious History

I joined my religious group on (date) _____

   at (name of church, synagogue, or other place of worship) _____

   in (city and state or province) _____

Name of present place of worship _____

Address:

   Number and street _____

   City and county _____

   State or province and Zip Code _____

I have been a member of my present place of worship since _____

Include photos of your baptism, confirmation, bar or bas mitzvah, church or synagogue, and special religious events. Write about religious classes, choir, and other activities.

My Schools

Write in your school names, addresses, colors, mascots, and teachers;
your favorite subjects, friends, awards, clubs, and dates of graduation.

Nursery school _____

_____

Kindergarten _____

_____

Elementary school _____

_____

_____

_____

Junior high school _____

_____

_____

High school _____

_____

_____

_____

Put photos of your schools and school events here.

My Favorite Things

Write about, draw, or paste in photos of toys, pets, books, stories, movies, sports, hobbies, clubs, and activities.

My Special Pages

Attach newspaper articles and photos of yourself and your family. Note dates, names, and events.

My Special Pages

(continued)

My Father

Photo here

Name _____

Date of birth _____

Place of birth _____

His father's name _____

His mother's name _____

Whom he was named after _____

_____

Date and place of marriage _____

_____

Occupation and place of employment _____

_____

Color of eyes _____ Color of hair _____

Hobbies and sports _____

_____

_____

_____

Interesting facts about him _____

_____

_____

_____

_____

_____

_____

My Mother

Name _____

Date of birth _____

Place of birth _____

Her father's name _____

Her mother's name _____

Whom she was named after _____
_____

Occupation and place of employment ____
_____
_____

Photo here

Color of eyes _____   Color of hair _____

Hobbies and sports _____

_____

_____

_____

_____

Interesting facts about her _____

_____

_____

_____

_____

_____

_____

_____

_____

My Brothers and Sisters

These people are your closest relatives, even closer than your mother and father. Only you and they have the same parents, the same grandparents, the same aunts and uncles and cousins.

Photo here

Name _____

Address:

   Number and street _____

   City and county _____

   State or province and Zip Code _____

Date of birth _____

Place of birth _____

Named after _____

Married to _____

   on _____ at _____

Occupation _____

Color of eyes _____ Color of hair _____

Hobbies and sports _____

_____

_____

_____

_____

Interesting facts _____

_____

_____

_____

My Brothers and Sisters

(continued)

Name _____

Address:

   Number and street _____

   City and county _____

   State or province and Zip Code _____

Date of birth _____

Place of birth _____

Named after _____

Married to _____

   on _____ at _____

Occupation _____

Color of eyes _____ Color of hair _____

Hobbies and sports _____

_____

_____

_____

_____

Interesting facts _____

_____

_____

_____

_____

Photo here

My Brothers and Sisters

(continued)

Photo here

Name _____

Address:

Number and street _____

City and county _____

State or province and Zip Code _____

Date of birth _____

Place of birth _____

Named after _____

Married to _____

on _____ at _____

Occupation _____

Color of eyes _____ Color of hair _____

Hobbies and sports _____

_____

_____

_____

Interesting facts _____

_____

_____

_____

My Brothers and Sisters

(continued)

Name _____

Address:

  Number and street _____

  City and county _____

  State or province and Zip Code _____

Date of birth _____

Place of birth _____

Named after _____

Married to _____

  on _____ at _____

Occupation _____

Color of eyes _____ Color of hair _____

Hobbies and sports _____

_____

_____

_____

_____

Interesting facts _____

_____

_____

_____

_____

Photo here

My Brothers and Sisters

(continued)

Photo here

Name _____

Address:

    Number and street _____

    City and county _____

    State or province and Zip Code _____

Date of birth _____

Place of birth _____

Named after _____

Married to _____

    on _____ **at** _____

Occupation _____

Color of eyes _____ **Color of hair** _____

Hobbies and sports _____

_____

_____

_____

Interesting facts _____

_____

_____

_____

_____

My Brothers and Sisters

(continued)

Name _____

Address:

    Number and street _____

    City and county _____

    State or province and Zip Code _____

Date of birth _____

Place of birth _____

Named after _____

Married to _____

    on _____ at _____

Photo here

Occupation _____

Color of eyes _____ Color of hair _____

Hobbies and sports _____

_____

_____

_____

_____

Interesting facts _____

_____

_____

_____

_____

My Paternal Grandfather

Your paternal relatives are the ones on your father's side of your family.
Thus your paternal grandfather is your father's father.

Photo here

Name _____

Address:

    Number and street _____

    City and county _____

    State or province and Zip Code _____

Date of birth _____

Place of birth _____

Named after _____

His father's name _____

His mother's name _____

Married on _____ **at** _____

Died on _____

Color of eyes _____ **Color of hair** _____

Hobbies and sports _____

_____

_____

_____

Interesting facts _____

_____

_____

_____

My Paternal Grandmother

Name _____

Address:

    Number and street _____

    City and county _____

    State or province and Zip Code _____

Date of birth _____

Place of birth _____

Named after _____

Her father's name _____

Her mother's name _____

Photo here

Died on _____

Color of eyes _____ Color of hair _____

Hobbies and sports _____

_____

_____

_____

_____

Interesting facts _____

_____

_____

_____

_____

My Maternal Grandfather

Your maternal relatives are those on your mother's side of your family.
Thus your maternal grandfather is your mother's father.

Photo here

Name _____

Address:

    Number and street _____

    City and county _____

    State or province and Zip Code _____

Date of birth _____

Place of birth _____

Named after _____

His father's name _____

His mother's name _____

Married on _____ **at** _____

Died on _____

Color of eyes _____ **Color of hair** _____

Hobbies and sports _____

_____

_____

Interesting facts _____

_____

_____

My Maternal Grandmother

Name _____

Address:

   Number and street _____

   City and county _____

   State or province and Zip Code _____

Date of birth _____

Place of birth _____

Named after _____

Her father's name _____

Her mother's name _____

Photo here

Died on _____

Color of eyes _____ Color of hair _____

Hobbies and sports _____

_____

_____

_____

_____

Interesting facts _____

_____

_____

_____

_____

My Great-Grandparents

Paternal Grandfather's Parents

Great-grandfather's name _____

Date of birth _____ Place of birth _____

His father's name _____

His mother's name _____

Married on _____ at _____

Died on _____ at _____

Interesting facts _____

_____

_____

_____

_____

Great-grandmother's name _____

Date of birth _____ Place of birth _____

Her father's name _____

Her mother's name _____

Died on _____ at _____

Interesting facts _____

_____

_____

_____

My Great-Grandparents
Paternal Grandmother's Parents

Great-grandfather's name _____

Date of birth _____ Place of birth _____

His father's name _____

His mother's name _____

Married on _____ at _____

Died on _____ at _____

Interesting facts _____

_____

_____

_____

_____

Great-grandmother's name _____

Date of birth _____ Place of birth _____

Her father's name _____

Her mother's name _____

Died on _____ at _____

Interesting facts _____

_____

_____

_____

My Great-Grandparents
Maternal Grandfather's Parents

Great-grandfather's name _____

Date of birth _____ Place of birth _____

His father's name _____

His mother's name _____

Married on _____ at _____

Died on _____ at _____

Interesting facts _____

_____

_____

_____

_____

Great-grandmother's name _____

Date of birth _____ Place of birth _____

Her father's name _____

Her mother's name _____

Died on _____ at _____

Interesting facts _____

_____

_____

_____

_____

My Great-Grandparents

Maternal Grandmother's Parents

Great-grandfather's name _____

Date of birth _____ Place of birth _____

His father's name _____

His mother's name _____

Married on _____ at _____

Died on _____ at _____

Interesting facts _____

_____

_____

_____

_____

Great-grandmother's name _____

Date of birth _____ Place of birth _____

Her father's name _____

Her mother's name _____

Died on _____ at _____

Interesting facts _____

_____

_____

_____

_____

My Family Tree

Fill in the names and dates of birth and death for each person. The "child" leaves are for you and your brothers and sisters. If you need more room, draw extra leaves near the trunk.

Great-great-grandmother

Great-great-grandfather

Great-great-grandmother

Great-grandmother

Great-grandfather

Great-great-grandfather

Grandmother

Great-great-grandmother

Great-grandmother

Great-great-grandfather

Father

Grandfather

Great-great-grandmother

Great-grandfather

Paternal

Great-great-grandfather

Child

Child

Child

The Family of

_____

(Your name)

My Extended Family

Aunts, Uncles, Cousins, Nephews, and Nieces

Although it does not occur as frequently now as it once did, families sometimes live together in large groups, with grandparents, aunts, uncles, and cousins sharing the same house or apartment. One person, often the oldest man or woman, is considered the head of the house. This person makes all the decisions for the rest of the family, even who should go to school or stay home and work, and who should marry whom.

In the following table, write the names and give the other information requested for all of your relatives, whether or not they live with you.

Name	Relationship	Date and Place of Birth	Address

My Extended Family

(continued)

Name	Relationship	Date and Place of Birth	Address

My Immigrant Ancestors

Your ancestors are the relatives from whom you are directly descended—your parents, grandparents, great-grandparents, great-great-grandparents, and so on. An immigrant is someone who enters a country that is not his or her native land and remains there permanently. Find out how your immigrant ancestors came to your country. Did they travel alone or in groups? Find out the name of the ships or planes your ancestors traveled on and the places (usually ports) and dates of entry. When you have this information, you can locate some immigrants' names on ships' passenger lists, which are available at some libraries and the National Archives.

Name of immigrant _____

From the city of _____ in the country of _____

Date of arrival _____ on the ship or plane _____

Settled in (city) _____ (state or province) _____

Occupation _____

Why the immigrant came to this country _____

Interesting facts _____

_____

Name of immigrant _____

From the city of _____ in the country of _____

Date of arrival _____ on the ship or plane _____

Settled in (city) _____ (state or province) _____

Occupation _____

Why the immigrant came to this country _____

Interesting facts _____

_____

My Immigrant Ancestors

(continued)

Name of immigrant _____

From the city of _____ in the country of _____

Date of arrival _____ on the ship or plane _____

Settled in (city) _____ (state or province) _____

Occupation _____

Why the immigrant came to this country _____

Interesting facts _____

_____

Name of immigrant _____

From the city of _____ in the country of _____

Date of arrival _____ on the ship or plane _____

Settled in (city) _____ (state or province) _____

Occupation _____

Why the immigrant came to this country _____

Interesting facts _____

_____

Name of immigrant _____

From the city of _____ in the country of _____

Date of arrival _____ on the ship or plane _____

Settled in (city) _____ (state or province) _____

Occupation _____

Why the immigrant came to this country _____

Interesting facts _____

_____

Autographs

Ask all your relatives to sign their names on this page. A signature is a way to identify a person.

Brothers _____

_____

_____

Sisters _____

_____

_____

Father _____

Mother _____

Paternal grandfather _____

Paternal grandmother _____

Maternal grandfather _____

Maternal grandmother _____

Great-grandparents _____

_____

Uncles _____

_____

_____

Aunts _____

_____

_____

Cousins _____

_____

My own signature _____

Family Stories

Write down your favorite family stories. Next to each story put the name of the person who told it to you and the approximate date that you heard it.

_____

_____

_____

_____

_____

_____

_____

_____

_____

_____

Draw or paste in pictures to illustrate the family story that you like most of all.

Family Reunions and Picnics

Write about family gatherings, who attended them, and when and where they were held.

_____

_____

_____

_____

_____

_____

_____

_____

_____

_____

Paste in photos of a family get-together.

Important People
from My Ancestral Homelands

There are many movie stars, politicians, and TV and sports personalities whose ancestors came from the same countries yours did. Many times these people changed their names, a little or a lot, to make them sound more "American," which, in this case, usually meant to make them sound more like English names. Often names were changed by government officials at the port of entry. Do you know of any famous persons who have the same ancestry as you? Write their names on this chart.

Name	Real Name	Ancestral Country

My Geography Pages

Draw or cut out a map of your immigrant ancestors' homelands, and show which cities or areas they came from.

My Geography Pages

(continued)

Find and paste in pictures or photos of people wearing the costumes of your ancestors' homelands.

Words I Have Learned in My Ancestors' Native Languages

Unless your ancestors came from an English-speaking country, their native languages were the languages they spoke when they arrived in this country. Most immigrants had a great deal of difficulty understanding officials and businessmen. Because of this, many immigrants formed small communities within a city, where almost everyone spoke the same language. In such a community, they could do almost all their business without a word of English. There were butchers, bakers, grocers, haberdashers, undertakers, and others who set up shop in the neighborhood to serve their former countrymen. Most of your immigrant ancestors, however, were probably employed in factories and businesses outside their neighborhood where English was the principal language.

Language	Foreign Word	English Meaning

Words I Have Learned in
My Ancestors' Native Languages

(continued)

Language	Foreign Word	English Meaning

Would you like to learn more of these languages someday? _____

Who taught you these words? _____

Ethnic Foods I Eat

People in other parts of the world do not all eat the same things we do.
Your ancestors prepared very special foods for different occasions.

Does your family eat any special ethnic foods? _____

What countries do these foods come from? _____

Explain what these foods are, list all the ingredients, and say when they are eaten. _____

_____

_____

_____

_____

_____

Draw pictures or paste in photos of your family's ethnic foods.

Do you have any ethnic cookbooks? _____

Write a favorite recipe here.

Ethnic Crafts I Have Learned

Do your ancestral countries have any famous special crafts? _____

What are they? _____

Have you learned to do any of these crafts? _____

Who taught you how to do these crafts? _____

Do these crafts come from a special area within your ancestors' homelands? _____

What is the name of the special area? _____

Describe the ethnic crafts you know and say what materials are used and what

procedures are followed. _____

_____

_____

_____

_____

Draw or paste in a photo of an ethnic craft project that you have made.
If possible, mount a sample of your work.

Folk Songs and Dances
from My Ancestral Homelands

Beautiful songs and dances originated centuries ago in many countries. Many of them are still performed today. Some of these songs and dances have found their way to this country.

Make a list of all the songs that you know from your ancestral homelands.

_____   _____

_____   _____

_____   _____

_____   _____

Have you ever seen folk dancers from your ancestral homelands perform? _____

What was the group's name? _____

When and where did you see the group? _____

Can you do any of the dances from your ancestral homelands? _____

Paste in a photo of yourself or of a group of folk dancers performing a traditional dance.

Ethnic Holiday Celebrations and Customs

Many families follow traditions from the "old country" when they celebrate holidays and special events.

Does your family have any ethnic celebrations? _____

When do these celebrations take place? _____

Describe these celebrations and say how they originated in your ancestral homelands.

_____

_____

_____

_____

_____

_____

_____

_____

_____

_____

Paste in photos of your family's ethnic celebrations.

Visits to
My Ancestors' Homelands

What countries did your ancestors come from? _____

Have you ever been to these places? _____

Would you like to go sometime? _____

Write about what you would like to see and do on a trip to your ancestral homelands.

_____

_____

_____

_____

Do you know anyone who lives in your ancestral homelands? _____

Do you write to anyone there? _____

Have any of your relatives ever visited your ancestral countries? _____

If so, talk to them about their trip. Ask them if you may have copies of photos from their trip. Paste these photos in here. Also paste in photos or pictures of things you would like to see.

Sample Page of Notebook Filing System

Make up a page like this one for every relative for whom you have any information. File the pages in a loose-leaf binder.

Name _____
        (Last)   (First)   (Middle)   (Maiden, if applicable)

Addresses, past and present _____

Born _____
        (Date)   (Place)   (Birth certificate: registration number and place)

Died _____
        (Date)   (Place)   (Death certificate: registration number and place, age, and cause)

Buried _____
        (Date)   (Cemetery)   (Grave location)

Baptized _____
          (Date)   (Place)   (Godparents)

Bar or bas mitzvahed _____
                        (Date)   (Place)

Immigrated into this country _____
                        (Date)   (From)   (To)   (Ship or plane)

Military service _____
                    (Country)   (Dates)   (Branch)

Schools attended _____

Married _____
          (Date)   (Place)   (Witnesses)

Spouse _____
        (Name)   (Born)   (Died)   (Parents)

Children: _____
          (Name)   (Born)   (Died)   (Married)

          (Name)   (Born)   (Died)   (Married)

Parents:
   Father _____
          (Name)   (Born)   (Died)   (Married)

   Mother _____
          (Name)   (Born)   (Died)

Brothers and sisters: _____
                        (Born)   (Died)   (Married)

          (Name)   (Born)   (Died)   (Married)

Use the reverse side of the sheet of notebook paper for public, church, and miscellaneous records, including information from city directories, the census, and gravestones.

Heraldry

Heraldry is the practice of designing and granting coats of arms, which are colorful symbols placed on shields. These battle shields were formerly worn in combat to distinguish allies from enemies. Most European countries began to grant coats of arms around the year 1200 A.D. They were given to men who distinguished themselves in battle or in other noble activities. Only the direct male descendants of these men are entitled to these coats of arms. No one has a right to use a design just because his last name is the same as one associated with a coat of arms. To bear a coat of arms, it must be proven through genealogy that a person is a descendant of the original bearer.

Heraldry is very complicated; you may want to read a few books on the subject (see the section Books to Help You). Coats of arms, as well as all noble titles (Sir, Baron, Duke, Prince, and so forth), are not recognized officially in the United States.

Great Britain has an active heraldry office, which allows people to design their own coats of arms and register them, for a fee. Many people choose symbols of their occupation or hobbies, pictures that remind them of where they live, and, for mottoes, English translations of foreign names or phrases.

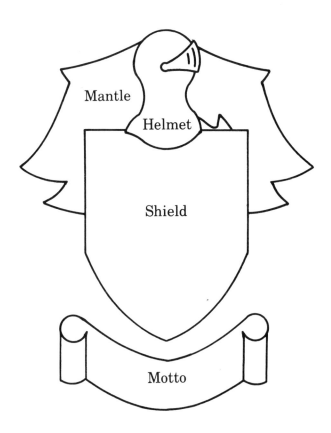

Heraldry

(continued)

Design your own coat of arms. Use the traditional colors of heraldry: white (which represents silver metal), yellow (which represents gold metal), red, green, blue, purple, and black. Make up a family motto too. Traditionally mottoes were in Latin or the bearer's native language. You may use English, if you wish.

Pedigree Charts

Here is one of the standard forms that genealogists use. You are number 1. Your father is number 2. Your mother is number 3. A father is two times his child's number. A wife is one more than her husband. Thus all men are even numbers, and all women are odd numbers.

b = Born
d = Died
m = Married

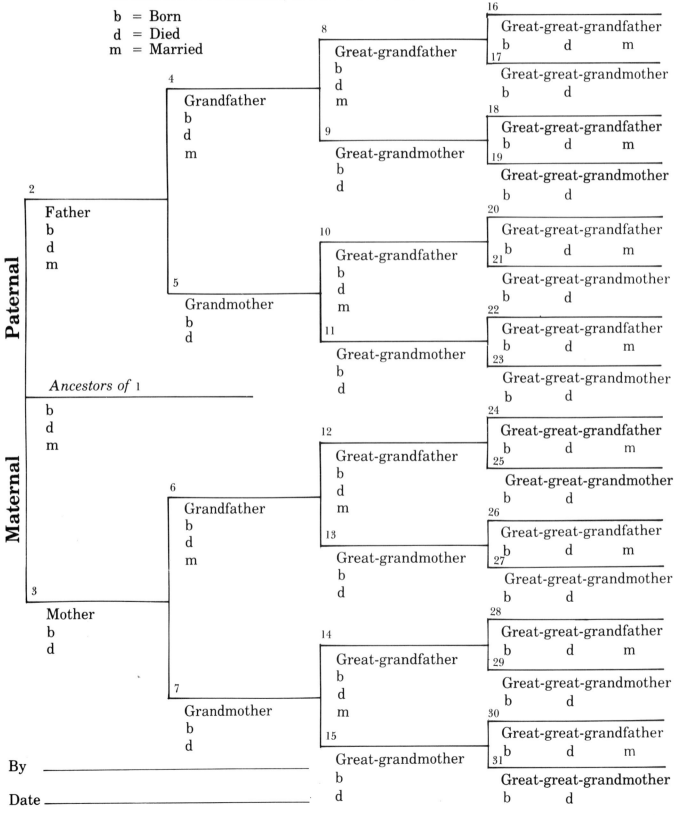

By _____

Date _____

Pedigree Charts

(continued)

Genealogists use only direct or *lineal* ancestors (parents, grandparents, great-grandparents, and so on), never *collateral* relatives (aunts, uncles, great-aunts, cousins), on their pedigree charts. You can make a chart of your own, however, that shows all of your relatives, including collateral ones. Use a large sheet of paper (from an art-supply store) or a piece from a roll of paper, such as blank computer print-out paper. The advantages of doing research on collateral relatives are that you get a good picture of family life as it used to be, and the more relatives you have to work with, the easier it is to verify parentage in cases where it is lacking in another record. For each person appearing on your pedigree chart, show his or her first and last names (maiden names for women) and dates of birth and death. For example:

John Brown
b. 4 July 1871
d. 7 September 1936

Note that on the sample pedigree chart, in keeping with current genealogical practice, the prefix *grand* is never used before *uncle* or *aunt*. Your father's brother is your uncle, but your grandfather's brother is your great-uncle and your great-grandfather's brother is your great-great-uncle.

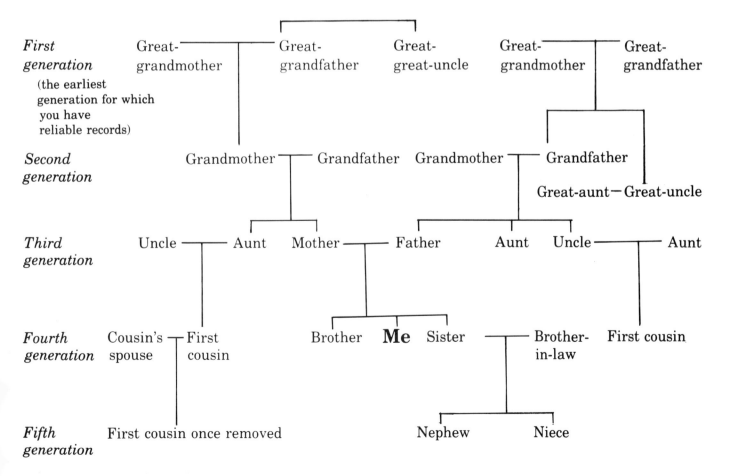

Correspondence

You will be writing many letters in your research. These letters fall into two categories: letters to interview relatives, and letters to obtain records and official documents.

You might like to get yourself some nice stationery with matching envelopes. You will also need slightly smaller envelopes that fit inside the other envelopes so that the people you write to can send you a reply. Get a supply of postage stamps too.

All correspondence requires neat, readable handwriting or typewriting; courteous, respectful language; correct spelling and proper grammar; and a complete presentation of all the important information you have about the subject. Keep your letters short. Always enclose a self-addressed, stamped envelope (the smaller one). This means you should address the smaller envelope to yourself and put a stamp on it.

You do not need the reply envelope if you are writing to a government office. The government will pay the return postage. The government will also charge a small fee to copy a document. Usually you will have to fill out a form with as much information as you have. Write to the proper government office and request several forms. Inquire what the fee is.

When writing to relatives, you might like to use the following format:

     Introduction
     Statement of purpose of letter
     Request for help
     Thank you
     Statement of willingness to share information
     Closing and signature

Your request may be in the form of a fill-in-the-blank inquiry. Leave space after each question for the person to answer. A follow-up thank-you note may be appropriate for a person who has spent a considerable amount of time with your request, or who sent you extra material, such as photographs or copied documents.

Keep a log of your correspondence. You may wish to use the following format.

Date and to Whom Sent	Information Requested and Fee if Applicable	Date Reply Received and Results

Where to Get Help

Relatives

Interview parents, aunts, uncles, grandparents, older and distant relations, and friends of the family. Ask to see their scrapbooks, photo albums, family bibles, diaries, and baby books. Ask permission to have copies made of any photos that you would like for your family album.

Public Libraries—Genealogy and Local History Departments

Libraries have maps, city directories, newspaper clippings, old newspapers, obituary files, and much more, although holdings depend on individual library policies. Librarians can direct you to the proper place to obtain a certain record. There are many addresses on file of places to write for information or documents.

State Bureaus of Vital Statistics

You can get copies of birth and death certificates, for a fee. Forms are usually available. Addresses can be found at the library. A birth certificate will usually give name, date and place of birth, and parents' names, ages, residence, and possibly occupations. A death certificate will usually list name, date and place of birth, age, occupation, residence, cause of death, burial place, undertaker, and parents' names and places of birth.

Church Records

These can be very helpful and sometimes more accurate than civil (government) registration records. Records are usually kept by the pastor or someone in the church office. It is best to make a phone call first to ask permission to see the records and explain what you are doing. These records are private and not open to public inspection, but if you are polite and act maturely, the pastor may help you. It is also possible to send your request by mail, but this should be done only when the church is too far to visit personally.

Cemetery Records

There is much information to be found in the cemetery office, if records have been kept carefully. Record books may show name, address, age, church affiliation, cause of death, date of burial, undertaker, and grave location. Many graves do not have markers, so check with the office for information. Officials can also show you where to find the graves you would like to see. Copy everything as it appears on the marker, even mistakes. You can also photograph markers or make rubbings.

Federal Census Records

In the United States, a census has been taken every ten years, starting in 1790. You may find such information as names, ages, places of birth, addresses, occupations, relationships, and more, depending on which census records you look at. Start with the more recent ones and work backward. The more recent the census records are, the more information they will contain. Anyone can see the records from 1790 to 1910. All the rest, from 1920 to the present, are not open to the public in order to protect the privacy of American citizens.

Many public libraries have microfilms of the census records for their state or local area. Your librarian can give you more information.

County Courthouses

You can search for vital records, wills, land records, naturalization records, and the like at the courthouse, which is located in the county seat. Call before your planned visit to find out if what you want is there, in what department it is located, and whom you should see.

Historical and Genealogical Societies

Historical and genealogical societies sometimes have collected old courthouse records, gravestone inscriptions, and other interesting materials. They will gladly help you. A historical society is interested in understanding the history of a particular locality by preserving and collecting information about old buildings, artifacts, and records of past events. A genealogical society promotes the study of family histories. Members share experiences and helpful hints on how to locate data. These groups often sponsor workshops and guest speakers who are knowledgeable in specific areas. Details about these organizations are available at the public library.

Church of Jesus Christ of Latter-day Saints (Mormon) Library

The members of the Mormon Church are very interested in genealogy and the preservation of records. All of their records are on microfilm and kept in Salt Lake City. Check your phone book to see if there is a branch near you, or write to Salt Lake City to ask for the nearest branch library. Each branch has a copy of the card catalog on microfilm. Mormons also have many county, state, federal, and foreign records. When you do find a group of records that you would like to see, copy the microfilm reel numbers from the index, give the numbers to the librarian, and she will order the microfilm from Salt Lake City. The microfilm will be sent to the branch library; all you pay is postage. Ordinarily, microfilm is lent for four weeks, but for a small additional fee, the period may be extended. A person does not have to be a member of the church to use the libraries or microfilms.

Here is the address for the main library:

Genealogy Department
Church of Jesus Christ of Latter-day Saints
50 East North Temple Street
Salt Lake City, Utah 84150

More Things to Do

Autobiography

Write about your life. Tell about amusing or interesting events. Use photos to illustrate vacations or important events. In some schools this is a class project. Ask your mother and father if they wrote one. My brief autobiography appears on page 56.

Scrapbook

Collect newspaper articles about your own or relatives' weddings, birth announcements, graduations, awards, obituaries, school pictures, report cards, programs, favorite people, scientific discoveries, bumper stickers, and similar things.

Photograph Album

Make up your own family photograph album. Sort out all the photos your family owns and label them on the back. Ask relatives for interesting pictures of weddings, grandparents when they were young, older ancestors, and anything else that will help build your knowledge of your family tree. Make copies of the pictures and return the originals to the owners. Always label the picture: who is in it, what is the event, and what is the date.

Autograph Album

Autograph albums were popular years ago. Start one of your own by asking all your relatives to write a few lines and sign their names and the date. Years from now the album will be interesting to read.

Family Tree with Names

Get some good art paper and a large, glass-covered frame. Use a light color paper for the background. Cut out a tree trunk from brown paper. Make a pattern for a leaf, and use it to trace on green paper. Cut out lots of leaves. On each leaf, print neatly (or use press-on letters, which you can purchase from a drafting supply store) the name, date of birth, and, if deceased, the date of death for each person on your family tree. Your name can be on the trunk of the tree, or next to your brothers' and sisters' as small branches off the trunk. Arrange all the leaves, starting near the trunk with your parents. From each of them, attach their parents, and so on. Put your family's name at the top or bottom to serve as a title. See the model on pages 26–27.

Family Tree with Photos

Make a tree like the one described in the preceding section, but also cut out branches. Then cut out a round or oval pattern and use it to trace the outlines of photos of your relatives' heads. Cut out the photos and paste them where leaves should be on the tree. Write each person's name below his or her picture.

Family Tree with Names and Photos

Make a tree like the first one described above, but use a larger frame. Arrange the photos (rectangles are best for this one) in rows in the space below the tree trunk. Label the photos if you wish. My family tree appears on page 57.

Newspaper Headlines on the Day You Were Born

Go to the library and ask to see the newspaper for the day you were born. Photocopy the front page, if you are allowed. Put the copy in your scrapbook or autobiography. Read all of the newspaper and look at the advertisements.

Photos of Old Homesteads

Get your camera and take pictures of homes that you and your parents and grandparents used to live in. Ask them to tell you their locations and any stories associated with them. Invite them to come along too. If some of the places are out of town, maybe someday your family will take a trip there. Don't forget to photograph buildings that your family owned. Take pictures of places of worship and schools members of your family attended.

Gravestone Rubbings

Many old gravestones are ornate and beautiful. Get large pieces of strong paper and black crayons from your art-supply store. Lay the paper on the stone and tape it down with adhesive or masking tape. Be careful not to move the paper when rubbing. Now rub the crayon over the surface of the paper; it will pick up the raised designs. Depressions will remain uncolored. If you prefer, you can simply copy the inscriptions, or photograph the gravestones.

Ancestral Country Scrapbook

Collect anything you can find about your ancestors' countries of origin, and make a scrapbook for each country.

Pen Pal

Write to a pen pal in one of your ancestors' countries. Many children in other countries are encouraged to learn other languages besides their own, and many choose English. It might be even more fun to write to a relative of yours who is your own age. Ask family members if they know anyone living in the "old country."

Books to Help You

is book is only the beginning. There are many
books that will help you expand your research
techniques and guide you to the proper source
material. Some of these books are written especially for young people. Most of them are easily
understood by anyone. A few are standard refer-
ence books with important information and can
be found in most public libraries. Keep a log of all
the books on genealogy you read, and be sure to
write down notes and comments.

Colket, Meredith B., and Frank E. Bridgers. *Guide
to Genealogical Records in the National Archives.* Washington, D.C.: U.S. Government
Printing Office, 1964.

Doane, Gilbert H. *Searching for Your Ancestors:
The How and Why of Genealogy.* Fourth edition.
University of Minnesota Press, 1973.

Grant, Francis J., editor. *The Manual of Heraldry.*
Reprint edition. Edinburgh: John Grant, Book-
sellers, 1962.

Hilton, Suzanne. *Who Do You Think You Are?
Digging for Your Family Roots.* Philadelphia:
Westminster Press, 1976.

National Office of Vital Statistics. *Where to Write
for Birth and Death Records.* Washington, D.C.:
Public Health Service, Department of Health,
Education, and Welfare, 1967.

———. *Where to Write for Divorce Records.* Washington, D.C.: Public Health Service, Department of Health, Education, and Welfare, 1965.

———. *Where to Write for Marriage Records.*
Washington, D.C.: Public Health Service, Department of Health, Education, and Welfare,
1965.

Neagles, James C. *Locating Your Immigrant
Ancestor.* Logan, Utah: Everton Publishers,
1975.

Pine, Leslie G. *American Origins.* Garden City,
New York: Doubleday, 1960.

Pottinger, Don, and Iain Moncreiffe. *Simple Heraldry.* New York: Mayflower Books, 1979.

Glossary

Alien: a person who was neither born in, nor is
now a citizen of, this country

Ancestor: a relative who lived before you; a parent, grandparent, great-grandparent, and so
forth

Archives: a collection of records

Autobiography: the story of a person's life
written by him or herself

Census: an official survey of all the people who
live in a designated area

City directory: a listing, in book form and usually published yearly, of city residents by name,
address, and occupation

Civil records: documents and other information kept by the government

Civil registration: the official acknowledgment
of the existence of certain documents or information

Descendant: a person who comes after another
related person; an offspring, a child, a grand-
child or great-grandchild, and so on

Emigrant: a person who leaves his homeland,
never to return to live there permanently

Ethnic: describing a group of people with the
same language and customs, or with the same
"roots"

Hereditary: possessing something either through
inheritance or by reason of birth

Immigrant: a person who enters a new country
to live there permanently, never returning to
his homeland

Line of descent: the series of a person's direct
forebears—parents, grandparents, great-
grandparents, and so on

Maiden name: a woman's last name before she
is married; her father's surname

Maternal: the mother's side of the family

Native country: place of birth

Naturalization: a process granting citizenship
to an alien or foreigner

Obituary: a short biography of a recently deceased person, usually published in newspapers

Passenger list: a list submitted to authorities
at the port of entry, and sometimes at the port
of departure, of all people traveling on board a
certain ship

Paternal: the father's side of the family

Pedigree: a family tree; a record of one's ancestry

Surname: a person's last name or family name

Vital statistics: records about birth, marriage,
and death

Rosemary's Autobiography

My name is Rosemary A. Chorzempa. My maiden name is Dembinski. I live in Temperance, Michigan, with my husband Larry and our children Becky, Nancy, and Timothy. I received a Bachelor of Arts degree in chemistry from the University of Toledo, and have worked at the university library, the Toledo–Lucas County Library, and Sherwin-Williams Chemicals. Presently I am a housewife—and an author. I belong to the national chapter of the Polish Genealogical Society.

I began to work on my own family tree in 1966 as a teenager. People were always telling me they were related to my grandfather or some other relative, but they didn't know how. I wanted to find out. Now I know more about my family's relationships, customs, and history than anyone else. As an extension of my research, I now lecture about Beginning Genealogy and Polish Roots to youths and adults in the Toledo and Temperance area. My activities extend beyond genealogy. I coauthored a centennial anniversary book, *The First Hundred Years, 1875–1975: A History of St. Hedwig Parish, Toledo, Ohio.* My article on Polish Easter eggs appeared recently in *PolAmerica* magazine.

I also teach classes and give demonstrations in making pisanki. Pisanki are eggs decorated by a special Slavic technique, in which designs are drawn on a raw egg with beeswax and then dyed. My pisanki have won ribbons in our local Bedford Township art show. Ethnic crafts and genealogy projects, such as writing your autobiography, are discussed in this book.

Rosemary's Family Tree

Piotr Modrzynski

Julia Kaczkowski

Jan Dembinski

Marcyanna Rygielski

Jan Dembinski Sr. 1831 Nov. 28, 1921

Wladyslaw Komorowski

Maryanna Modrzynski Mar. 20, 1910 Feb. 24, 1980 Grzegorzefcol.

Walenty Pokrywka

Marianna Kiatkiewicz

Kazmierz Herwat 1809 Jul. 15, 1886

Anastazya Boracina

Izydor Komorowski Dec. 31, 1843 Nov. 31, 1933 Poznań,Pol.

Jan Dembinski Jr. Sep. 19, 1873 Feb. 24, 1960 Milwiec,Pol.

Janwiec Sr. Dec. 9, 1855 Jul. 6, 1955 Poznań, Pol.

Samuel Szulc 1849

Victoria Dudek Jul. 30, 1832 Aug. 8, 1904 Szubin, Pol.

Walenty Chudzinski

Maryanna Chudzinski 1844 Oct. 20, 1918 Żelaznej, Pol.

Katarzyna Herwat Nov. 5, 1850 May 16, 1909 Szubin, Pol.

Katarzyna

Francesca Komorowski Mar. 8, 1875 Feb. 23, 1959 Toledo, Oh.

Margaret Szulc Jun. 14, 1877 Dec. 14, 1972

Piotr Chorzempa

Tomasz Boczkowski

Karol Chorzempa Jan. 15, 1875 Apr. 25, 1954 Sokołow, Pol.

Julianna

Jan Chrostek

Jacob Rutkowski

Katarzyna Zagłewski

Franciszek Boczkowski Oct. 9, 1878 Feb. 1, 1962 Wolowa, Pol.

David John Stanley Dembinski Feb. 8, 1916 Toledo, Oh.

Helen Loretta Pokrywka Jul. 24, 1913 Toledo, Oh.

Franciszek Chrostek

Mary Walicki

Jozefa Pietrykowski

Kazmierz Rutkowski Feb. 15, 1856 Dec. 2, 1936 Miłosław, Pol.

Rozalia Marta Rutkowski Aug. 23, 1891 Sep. 16, 1962 Toledo,Oh.

Irene Rose Boczkowski Sep. 7, 1916 Toledo, Oh.

William Theodore Chorzempa Jun. 19, 1918 Toledo, Oh.

Agata Karolina Chrostek Feb. 3, 1889 Sep. 8, 1944 Sokołow,Pol.

Victoria Luzinski

Lukas Luzinski

Stanisław Piotrowski

Jozefa Piotrowski Sep. 1859 Oct. 4, 1924

Rose Mary Dembinski Feb. 27, 1951 Toledo, Oh.

RD + LC 1972

Lawrence Chorzempa May 2,1945 Toledo, Oh.

Anna Walicki

Marcianna Jakobiak Jan. 1832 May 9, 1923

Andrzej Jakobiak

| Bobby Jill Dick May 24, 1950 | + | Mark David Dembinski Apr. 24, 1954 | | Ronald Joseph Chorzempa Jul. 24, 1942 | + | Kathleen Ann Miller Jun. 12, 1951 | | Mary Ann Chorzempa Aug. 29, 1949 | + | Thomas Foxlee Mar. 20, 1948 |

Victoria Irene Mar. 11, 1981

Rebecca Rose Mar. 19, 1973

Nancy Rose Jul. 6, 1977

Timothy Lawrence Apr. 6, 1980

Kerrie Ann   Oct. 10, 1979

Sean   Oct. 15, 1970
Jennifer   Jul. 7, 1977
Heather   Aug. 27, 1978
Brian   Aug. 27, 1978

Vicki | Tim | Becky Rose | Nancy Rose | Thomas Sean | Jennifer Helene | Brian Wm. | Heather Colleen | Kerrie

Bobby Jill | Mark David | Rosemary | Larry | Mary Ann | Thom | Kathy | Ron

Rose Martha | Frank | Frances | John Dembinski Jr. | Irene Rose | David | Helen | Bill | Margaret | John Pokrywka | Agatha | Karl

Mary Komorowski | Isadore | Josephine | Cas. Rutkowski | Mary Dembinski | John Dembinski Sr. | Marianna Pokr.

Rosemary 1978

57